Amen to Artillery

Sean Lause

Cyberwit.net
HIG 45 Kaushambi Kunj, Kalindipuram
Allahabad - 211011 (U.P.) India
http://www.cyberwit.net
Tel: +(91) 9415091004
E-mail: info@cyberwit.net

Printed at Repro India Limited.

For my son, Christopher, with love

"…the wind blows hard from our past into our future and we are that wind, except that the wind's nature was not to last."

—John Berryman

Acknowledgements

I would like to thank Tom Beery and Will Wells for their wise advice as I wrote these poems.

Poems in *Amen to Artillery* have appeared in the following journals:

"Ancestral dance"
"Inheritance"

Toasted Cheese
The Innisfree Poetry Journal

"Thirst and meteors"
"Does the web imagine the spider?"

Writer's Journal
Sublunary Review

"Imagination longing"

California Quarterly, Green Hills Literary Lantern, Main Street Rag

"The knife sharpener"
"The antique children"

Scars Publication
Brief Wilderness, Blue Lake Review

"I knew a world once deeply in its wounds"
"The visitor"

Roanoke Review

FutureCycle Press

Preface:

A college creative writing professor once told our class: "Never write a poem about a dog or a grandmother." In this book, I took half of his advice. Nowhere in this collection will you find a single poem about a canine. My grandfather owned and ran the second-to-last general store in Ohio, the Yoder General Store and Grocery. When he became too old to work, my grandmother converted the store into an antique shop, The Old Country Store. I first entered the store at age seven, and my life was never the same afterwards. This is the story of that time of loss and wonder.

Contents

Preamble

Say God, then,
for why leads forever somewhere,
a breathing along the blood, or
memory of a memory mirrored
of treetops brushing the clouds,
or falling leaves spelling the wind
to the mind, fall-deep
in the old lost rooms of the past.
Forever some semblance of resemblance,
dreaming of possible worlds,
a wind to flow and flood low
through fields of weeds and wanders,
or silence between drops of rain
listening for a word to guide it
color to color, correlated patterns
in moonlit flowers, or the moon's
penciled sketches of the night.
I was forever disappearing,
speechless within all that everywhere,
counting the endlessing stars
that were mirrors of mirrors of mirrors,
and now the memories come
like fireflies weave darkness to light,
their golden call for response,
their messages gone as soon as it arrives,
forever beyond my reach.
And I in the forever glass,
in the grass of the fields,
the stars, the moon,
and my own wandering soul,
alive in the mystery.

Ancestral dance

Here is a photograph—
My grandparents dancing motionless
around their apple tree, deep-rooted,
their stone house planted solid
in their dreaming, fertile fields.
Their embrace whirls through time
to touch my name, my hands that
hold the picture like a breath a prayer,
this forever lost, this here as I
let myself enter the fading frame.
In distance the fields lie free, cut by the
merciful scythe, in the captured light
as I watch my ancestral lovers in their dance,
while the heavy honey bees find broken apples,
hang in them upside-down, cling and burrow.
A butterfly flutters by eternity,
in this endless flow of borrowed time,
as I see my mother, nine, reading
Wuthering Heights under the tree, caught
in a dream, not yet dreaming me.
All this is gone as yesterday Sundays,
futile to become again, and yet
so relentlessly present—this dance,
cupped in the palms, a moon charm
for the lunatic vanishings of time.

My mother's secret chancel

Twelve years old, my mother
built a private chancel in the woods,
made of two trees, a wooden plank,
a candle, and her love.
She was not alone there—
spiders wove old faces in the grass,
while bees pondered the air, circled,
alit, and burrowed to sweetness.
Oh my dear, your faith, your hallelujah:
Willows dream in willow longing,
turtles clasp whole in turtle love,
the way to the grass is through the grass,
the earth all heavens undone at last.

Inheritance

In the back of my grandmother's antique store,
I overhear my grandfather chanting:
"I don't want to die. I'm afraid to die."
And my grandmother soothes him, "I know, I know."
And she opens doors, drapes, blinds, and windows,
old glass lights in carillon colors,
and still he cries his fear of dying.
But I am five and the watches are asleep.
Clocks line the walls, each hushed at a separate hour.
This store is a theatre of light,
crystal air, tobacco scents, and hard-bound
books, clasped in secret knowledge.
And now her hands guide me to the garden,
and I am all lit crystal and sun,
as the world rehearses another day.
The light stings like shattered glass,
and broken strings are blowing in the trees.

The string that kept me from away

The disappearing are kids one by one:
Charlie Steman, hit by a truck
right in front of the crossing guard.
I watch the blood shoot from his nose
in a fountain, as if hating the earth,
as if trying to return to Christ.
Kevin Todd was born with a broken heart
no doctor could fix.
He *knew* he was going to die
some soon year, month, week
or day, and his only prophesy
came true as freezing rain, always telling
me he was going home to God,
but what home, or God, I never knew.
Other kids turn into empty chairs.
Little Mary Stapleton, a disease
none of us can pronounce
takes her whole, after turning her
face into a tambourine.
Mrs. Hellinger creeps like a crab
from window to window, peers
the horizon, screams "Here come
the Russian bombers!" And we dive
beneath our desks or hide inside
our lockers. But there is no escape.
One day three of us are gone
without a word—no—there were
whispers who got them—some man
in a yellow raincoat waiting after school

offering free candy, an open black bag
crouched behind him. Or vampires
that can float through your bedroom
window in a mist, teeth clicking
like plotting spiders in the dark.

We all know there is a schedule
for departure with each of our names, that
we are not allowed to see. "They're killing
the kids on Main Street!" But downtown
are only deaf windows, steel, and blind traffic.

The worst is the kid in my bedroom mirror
with the twisted neck like a bent paperclip,
feet caught in a bog, with a hellhound
closing in behind him. That kid beckons
me enter, says he loves me, so enter
my world of mirrors where you'll be home
forever.

I start to float around the house
late each night when the mice
are asleep, then out my bedroom window,
up to the knives of waiting stars.
I hang a blanket over the mirror,
but the hound tears it free,
then turns his red eyes on the boy.
Visiting with her grace of years,
my Grandmother ties a string
round my narrow wrist, tells me:
"If you feel yourself floating
away, just tug on this, and I
will reel you back to earth."
It works, for now, for now.
I am safe for once,
held to gravity by her ancient days.

One day in Lima, Ohio, 1963

Watching witches blow from tree to tree,
mysterious daylight, drear November's
bones protruding from a daymoon.
Dismissed too soon, I see the world
drift by dazed, song-less, and alone.
Every fallen leaf a demon's head.
Sphere-screams planet the cloud-wheel heavens,
smoke-ridden autumn turning into ghosts.
Schools closed, factories shut down, people frozen in time.
Can you read the buried faces where I tread?
A worm-eaten dwarf named Edgar follows me home,
enters the front door before me, locks me out
forever. A mobster sits on the front stairs next
to me, hands me his gun, weeping. I hear
my parents calling but I am long, long gone.
A hearse crawls near, sniffing for customers.
Can you remember where you were when
Gods were hidden in the stars?
When roses came blowing down the street of elms,
and all the world lost track of time.

My grandfather's funeral

My father kept me from viewing the casket,
the grave a grinning scar in rounded earth.
Now he retrieves a fallen oak leaf,
shows me its fragile veins,
like the veins in my arm, he takes my arm,
and holds the leaf to my veins.
"This is yours," he tells me,
and hands me the fallen leaf.
Later, in the car,
my mother gently pulls my
hand to hers.
"No, no" she whispers.
"Don't wave. Don't wave
to Grandmother."
I watch out the window
a gentle daymoon following
my grandmother's car
like an old man peering through a curtain.

I spy on my parents speaking of me

"I think he should spend time with Mother."
"It makes sense. She's alone now, and he seems lost."
"Did you talk to him about death?
"I showed him a leaf."
"You showed him a *leaf?*
"I didn't know what to say. What did you say?"
"I said it's just like going to sleep."
"Did it help?"
"No. Now he can't get to sleep."
"It started with that damn assassination."
"No. His grandfather. He heard something."
"I watched him after Dallas. He dragged his mattress down
from upstairs and jumped up and down
on it for three days."
"I know. Doctor Horack says he gave *himself* a fever."
"He's always been a nervous child."
"I think the country might help him."
"We may have to wait for Spring. The school."
"Let's ask him."
"He's troubled."
"I know."

Thirst and meteors

Seven years old, stunned by fever and nightmare,
the only cure, lie my fear in the grass
as my grandmother sought the orchard well
to draw the lonely water that could heal.
I watched the town's distant sparks,
her lantern swaying the apple boughs—
paused, then quivered under the earth
to the secret place where mystery and darkness meet.
Covenant of thirst and joy, green and amethyst,
came the first Spring meteors,
in paths of ecstatic sand returning time
in breathless words of whispered quest.
She drew the water, moon-silvered, moon-cooled,
her dress folding and unfolding, like memories,
poured the captured earth-blood, fingers touching mine
lightly as garden spiders weaving suns.
In the water's mirror I dreamed
ripening planets, conceiving moons,
pirate meteors scooping to hidden gold…
I drank until my heart awakened.
The slippered moon let down a light
that shivered every stone,
then folded in a wing of night,
and slept it gently home.

My grandmother's antique store by day

One's surrounds are, at first,
as simple as ascending through music,
memory and imagination
woven round the vision of a child.

My grandmother's antique store in the country,
where roads are not bent to geometry
but travel free like unstrung fates
passing by this store of fragile glass aglitter
dawn's light wanding goblets red to pink,
sunset to blue and gold, a stained glass
rainbow arcing from wall to wall,
transforming all my world.

A strange word: "antique."
Because this room is all alive to me,
the unwound clocks that line the walls,
each hand hushed to a time lost long ago.
A grandfather clock she winds to all the hours,
stirs, chirrs, like an old man clearing his throat,
then sends a golden gong to start the day.

In the front window, a Brown Bess flintlock,
cocked at some invisible enemy, a bullet
placed next to it, stained with old blood
from an old wound, old war, old world
gone long ago, yet pried in pain
from too-mortal flesh and bone.
A cash register with a gloved hand

pointing to "Change." Behind it,
a wooden telephone with a face
like a long-nosed man with silver eyebrows.

Time seems held so calmly here,
no threat, and loneliness a home, as I
sit in my grandfather's swivel chair
before his oak desk stuffed with letters
that will never be sent or read.

All I swirls in the scent of tobacco leaves,
and sunlight on old, stained wood,
smoothing my hands over the Tappan stove,
imagining the ghosts of farmers in the rocking chairs
he carved by hand, laughing and talking of crop yields,
while my grandfather played his harmonica
which was the size of an ear of corn.

Or I lean far over the soda pop machine,
my hand swirling the cold water, then letting it
grow still and deep, to see the green and blue bottles
like buried treasure to the diver's held breath.

Best of all are the rows and rows of books,
bound in soft leather, with gold-engraved names,
Compton's Encyclopedia, whose names I chant
each night as I drift to sleep: "Somewhere to Time",
"Unknown to Waterloo," and my favorite, "Amen
to Artillery." That book whispers secrets.
That book chants of peace.

My grandmother's antique store by night

A jewel
in the palm
of a velvet glove.

Chess board,
the pieces cool, poised
for war and chaos.

Eternity stains
these panes
of multi-colored glass.

The wand
of the Grandfather clock
the only motion.   ·

Japanese fans—
night moths
in the summermoon

The moon lights
goblets to green,
aqua, silver, silence.

Victorian dolls,
propped in a row,
eyes reflecting moons.

And I am silence
and darkness,
a breath, within the calm.

Wind, leaf shadows
gusting up the walls,
black ghosts beckoning.

Rocking horse
suspended from the ceiling,
rider invisible.

A spinning wheel
threading the night
with stars.

Ruy Lopez

Pray now what's that bishop doing here
worrying my poor gentle knight?
You move your pieces with a deft
flick of your wrists.
I move mine like bowling pins.
You are teaching me,
but I am one slow learner,
seeing patterns everywhere
like constellations conned from a book
that fade back to chaos with a blink.
You press your clock, I press mine.
You press your clock I slam mine.
Yours is smooth and certain.
Mine hides its face in shame.
I hate the thing, it wants me gone.
My encyclopedia lies open
to Austerlitz, my mad ambition—
learn chess from brilliant warfare,
Napoleon's plump rump up on Marengo,
besting all their armies at once.
But all my foolish troops retreat
like leaves blown by harsh October wind.
Patience, patience, you say, helping,
it's all in motion wedded to time.
I gulp-swallow. My whole left wing is gone!
My king gives me sideways looks,
pleading. He fears the encroaching,
approaching blackness. Try anything,

he whispers, sacrifice those useless
pawns. Kings are not bred to die.
But castles chime, too late, too late.
The walls are breached, artillery
gone. Your knights glide in
like murderous swans. My kingdom topples,
a crown too big for me to wear.

My king humbles face first in despair.
His queen mourns him with contempt.
Your hand—oh how I hate to grip it.
"You're learning," you reassure me.
But I am trapped here alone
on Saint Helena in my rage.

The farms at Yoder

Seed and sweat and sun and plow—
still earth hungers, still it thirsts
to be earth to its deepest roots,
in fields cut sharp as pencil shavings,
orange clay and black sod and crow shadows
black angels in the light.
Comes the rain, promising green and gold,
tree-tormenting storm with tarantula clouds
bending leaves to palings, shrouding
the sky-clock, and lowering the watch
of the moon, now deep night, scent of
mint, prodigy of thirst and origin.

Ode to the ruling wind

Come to me unruly, ruling wind,
teach my alone to endure the dark,
send the leaves to seek their meanings,
and send my fear to the patient stars.
Comfort me with your storms I love,
your haunted houses in the air!
Drown my rage and cool my fever,
and whirl my love beyond despair.
Teach the wheat to pray in whispers,
and bring the maddened hornet calm.
Bid the corn bow down in reverence,
and wind the world with your song.

The knife sharpener

A sharp blade's edge
will sing in the sun
under the sway of her steady hands
within whose grasp
such ancient learning lives.
She whistles, presses the pedal
as if playing an ancient organ.
The wheel and the earth turn
to her song of metal on stone,
and birds become the voices of the trees.
She guides the knife with care
until sparks overflow the wind.
The sun's blaze refines to a purity
down the cool edge of blue steel,
and the zodiac turns its menagerie of fate.
She strops the blade to a fine shine,
checks the edge shape with careful eye,
then tests its power on an apple,
slicing it neatly in halves, and tempted,
takes one half in one firm bite.

Watching a meteor shower

"Don't focus on any particular place
in the sky, or any particular time,"
my grandmother says. "Just lie back
and allow them to enter your field of vision."

So I watch the chancel stars, bell-blue,
or white, or silver, and wait in the field
for the sly, shy meteors to come
complicit with the night.

Now the first messenger from afar,
then more—firebird wings in flight,
unfolding in whispers or bright hissings,
sapphire incarnations of angel light.

We lie alone in the night's embrace,
scenting the grace of grasses, blessed
by fireflies that suture the darkness,
revealing then hiding their gold.

Under the paths of ecstatic flame,
under the tambourine moon,
Our "ahs!" of inbreath and exhale,
the sky more pure than prayer.
The meteors come and come, pulsing blood
and longing, bringing brief time from
eternity, blessed quest, silver serpents,
holy outriders of the fall.

I drift to sleep, my hand in hers,
the sky lit all blue-gentian,
the earth a gentle embrace of secrets,
the moon a compass rose of love.

A prayer for the moons of color and shade

Black moon, black moon,
not even shadows know your purity,
cloaked, disguised as night.
The lost and lonely know you from afar.
Grey moon, grey moon,
guides the wolf in search of prey.
The ice below his blue-cold paws
is a crystal of poisoned jewels.
Silvermoon, silvermoon,
spends itself in its cool alone.
Have you come to soothe my burning fever
with a spell from your magic coin?
Red moon, red moon,
your light bleeding from the stars,
here to remind me that each true vision
comes like a crucifixion.
Green moon, green moon,
my love, my favorite of all,
reflecting a world you can barely see,
in your dream of possibilities.
I pray for these moons, every
and all, I bless and affirm
and cry for their return. Without them,
I am merely empty sky.

The moon's way

The moon's wu-wei,
the white clover yearning for return,
and I, moon-lover, loved by this moon,
watch the ten thousand things
unfolding into night.
I lie on my back in the grass,
tracing the calligraphy of stars…
Were these hands
made to brush them free of dust?
Breaths of joy meteor trails.
This is the moon's sway,
counting its silver down to earth,
and when it sets, embracing darkness,
I rise and return,
dancing free of my shadow.

Flightfall

I leave the earth,
ascend to the light of lights,
pass the asteroid belt
that revolves endlessly in time
like shattered civilizations.
I learn that none of the planets,
not even Mars,
has ever heard of war,
and constellations patterned themselves
with no need of human help.
A crosstree guides me high and higher,
its course-sail unfolds the Milky Way.
Breathless before the eyes of God,
why need I descend to earth?
I am where I need to be.
Yet soon I fall between darkness and silence,
return to beginnings in the tumbling sky,
all this blue within the blue. Perhaps
this is my home after all, in love
with all this nearing green.

Does the web imagine the spider?

We need not wait for interpretations.
An ant is moving punctuation,
changing the sentence as it goes and goes.
A meaning cannot find itself,
but tree roots spider the earth with clues.
They have learned to clench down deep.
Spider illuminations await the dawn,
as each new web awaits its poem.
Wonder may be a form of patience.
Lucid illusions will find their own fate,
like intricate crickets design the dark.
Watch. Listen.
I follow each longing wind by wind,
the way gaps between stars
whisper the invisible.
It's a matter of precedence.
The wind unwinds the light in things.
There is no leaf that cannot trace the air.
It may be sudden,
this careful grace,
a silence that surrenders to devotion.

Call them all nightingales

—"Rather than deprive any bird of its song, to call them all nightingales." –William Carlos Williams

A white chicken,
a red barn—
and the space between.
The redbird calls,
and calls again,
bringing the distant rain.
Starling on a bare branch,
feathers dark and dusty.
Yet listen! It sings of heaven.
Song wren
invisible
as a soul.
Wild canary
perched
in chicory.
Owl
clutched to a branch,
watching the stars conspire.
A mourning dove,
what if
she is really singing praise?

Dragon song

Sunlight—
      humming—
bird
here
and
       back—
to heaven
cloud
and wind,
these roarers
weave a dragon
storms a castle
becomes whale
becomes a great
blackbird beneath
your eyelids
becomes electric
skeletons
dancing across the trees
then
descends to roots
become veins
invading your blood and dreams
and now you see
the dragon of the ten-thousand things,
and you are its claws of thunder,
your scales the centuries,
your fire the sun and stars,
until you fade,

and now your eyes
are two doves
enfolding the moon
till day returns with
the hummingbird,
and a sunlit
grass—hopp—er
in the green
empty mind.
The field a sudden gold.

Wild wren,
its song
a longing green

        Wheat in breeze
        curving
        like mermaids

                Long weeds,
                ears—
                rabbit!

Dragonfly
wings in sunlight,
radioactive blue

    Archon
    praying
    mantis

                Gold corn stalks
                watching
                their shadows

Intricate
crickets
invisible

And a heart
surprised
by tenderness

The seedpod mimosa

Bend your eye to its curve of light,
this seedpod engoldening the green
almost appears to be breathing.
How gently it cups itself
like a finger brushing free
a child's tear.
Balanced in mid-air,
an acrobat
suspended in time.
On the cusp of its fate
it bows in the rushing wind.
Does it long to feed the earth?
Or does it fear the fall?
Or both? Pregnant with seeds,
it is barely hanging on.
A question mark, or
parenthesis, parent
to an old mystery.

Imagination longing

The moon imagines itself
from silence to an O of wonder,
dreaming of how to spend its silver coin.
The earth is a faithful horse
circling its absent master's house.
The house weeps for the horse down its panes.
The sky is in love with the light it can't hold,
the light with the sun it remembers,
the sun a throbbing vacancy of blue.
Though they burn holes in darkness,
the stars forever shiver. The darkness
is a door longing for a key.
Planets ripen for a harvest
that never comes. Each dreams a world
beyond the endless zero of its sum.
One child day I tore a flower free,
and toppled from the all of holiness,
till I learned to bless the shadows of the Fall.

Firefly hymn

Sun sets, wheat cools,
you come again
to share your light with me,
the bowing corn your congregation.
I can hear that light
pulsing in my blood.
Were you woven from the stars?
You guide the darkness field to field.
Teach me to sing your silence.
A moving Christmas tree!
All heaven descending, blending
with the town's distant, blinking lights,
you, the tears of lost angels,
you the earth's throbbing love.

Giveth

God giveth
the increase,
the word seeds
scattered to stars,
the world pulse
felt along the blood,
or in flowers
unfolding into light,
careless of death
in the yielding air,
careful to seek
the only of your love.

Seashell

Lift this seashell from the poem.
Place it next your ear where beats its heart,
wave-whispered, shore-echoing,
and sound its star-song through your blood and breath.
Let the sacred spider of the stars
weave you in and out of time.
Call winds of light to reveal the silence
till your soul turns smooth as sand
blessing cries of pebbles on the shore,
all your words whirled with the earth's turn
to oceans that are tears of God.
Then return this shell
to the sea from which it fell,
those white sands of the Milky Way,
where one grain mirrors eternity.

Lightplay angel song

Angelus an old song sun anew,
renew our yesterdays, sky-carved
moon, alone I await your hidden faces.
Moonlit energy radiating glass
to glass, echoing colors, a chant
of beads, goblet to goblet, poured
full with your shimmering wine,
and sound like a distant tuning fork.
Rhyming light, light rhyming
with color, blue-whispered
to green to indigo and now—
sleep into darkness and silence
as moon sets, and stars retire,
awaiting the dawn of the new.
Comes the sun, longing for return,
turns the store kaleidoscope, till
each color molds its own emotion.
Now this light epitomizes,
threads from glass to glass
as thin and fragile as dragonfly wings.
It is a symphony of light,
a sea-surge carrying me far,
where sky and sea, moon and sun,
are blended into song.

Night spider

Each night
an ebony spider
spun gentle stars over my bed,
weaving new constellations,
her web cradling the light
until I no longer knew
if stars were spun from darkness
or the darkness from the light.
It did not seem
to matter much to her
as she lowered
each night on her string,
crept softly across my eye lashes,
and settled to sleep in my dreams.

The cry from night's destination

I lie awake awaiting its dark call,
its long lonely cry of longing
for something—mystery, enchantment
of distant lands, or perhaps
mere distance itself, in time or memory.
It comes again,
always at some odd, bent hour of the night,
stealing through the fields,
wings waving the wind back,
cry seeking my heart,
landing on the branch it owns,
demanding I watch its waiting eyes.
This old owl, master of darkness.
Its eyes gold coins.
(What they see or spend,
only the gods know).
Its call as rhythmic
as a heartbeat.
It watches and watches,
ever patient, my guide,
my guard.
While far away,
fireflies light their candles through the fields.

Waiting for the storm

I love the thunder coming
like a language we lost long ago,
my nerve ends electric, furious bees.
The first wind-gust icicles through my chest.
Treetops bow and graceful-wave.
The store listens in its antique veins,
blown shadows spooking down the aisles.
Sky skeletons tremble the earth's flesh.
Clouds conspire into dragons, thundering
encore more than thought can bear as
crows swirl like woeful leaves of exile.
At last the rain comes, shimmering knives
hidden in the cloak of twilight, this torment
weaves my blood with joy, as all the
sacred fields yield free their secrets.
Trace the notes that plunder down this harp,
fathom you, take you whole into the web.
Trust the wound, as fireflies suture night.
It heals in mornings radiant with suns.

Watching the antique store through a mir-ror-kaleidoscope

A poem absolute
invents a world
from a world,
weaving space through time,
bringing the all-color angels
down here where they belong.
Or perhaps the colors dozen
to a dazzle drinking light
till they lean on one another
for support like
friendly drunks then all
come bumbling tumbling home.
These sudden combinations
come from as far as nowhere
and near as an open door,
to catch a dreaming whole.
They forth and retreat, hide or
reveal themselves, like Munchkins.
Now spin and whirl yourself
until you become the kaleidoscope,
becoming something rare and strange,
all the known undone around you
as you revolve in a miracle of your own device,
ancient and ever new.

The Buyer

He strides up and down each aisle, all huff
and snort, making inspection, hair groomed and creamed,
fingers moving like tap-dancing spiders,
feet shod in creaseless shoes, shined to a sheen.
His blue eyes like drained swimming pools.
My grandmother walks slowly behind him,
patient, turning a toothpick in her mouth.
She knows the price of each item, and its worth.
I sit at my grandfather's desk, scowling,
as I watch this owl-faced man scan our store.
Now his hands are behind his back,
waving at me like crippled wings.
"Why are these clocks not running?" he asks.
"Because they only have hands," she replies.
He ignores her, eyes me. "I may buy one."
"You buy it, I'll wind it." Hiding a smile.
He snatches a blue angel, weighs it in his palm.
"Only glass," he sniffs, "Not crystal?"
"Just the memory."
"Memories don't sell in the market."
Silence.
He spots my grandfather's desk, then narrows
his eyes at me. "This is good. It looks good."
"It's hand-carved from one of our oaks."
"No, no, no. I mean it will fetch a good price."
Again he looks at me, annoyed now.
"Has this boy found Jesus?"
"Didn't know he was missing."
"Without Christ, the boy is lost."

"Everything here is lost and found."
He pays for his purchases, hands me
a bible the size of a biscuit, exits the front door,
calls his moving van up, taps his foot in the road,
shouts and curses at the clumsy movers.

I try to say to her, but I am voiceless:
"He doesn't understand. He's blind and deaf.
What I learned from Amen to Artillery—
Close eyes and ears for three seconds,
and empires topple and fall."
A Grandfather clock is lugged out,
and shoved in with his other possessions.
I sigh. Time has entered our world.

The toy soldier

He sports a rosy circle on each check,
sign of youthful health or budding plague.
He's so British in his bright-red uniform,
easy target, shako hat like a strange growth.
He greets me each day, eager for more blood.
I spread his world-map beneath him
and wind him up, in his left hand a sword,
his right tugging a tiny cannon.
His metal boots march from color to color.
Boundaries mean nothing to him.
All colors must be trod and trod to red.
Never smiles, all duty, mouth a razor-straight scar.
For a moment, he kingdoms each nation
as his own, but the key winds slowly down.
Night. Silence here is so very dark,
and he has so little else than war.

Captain Miracle: Neo-Colonialist

In second grade I wrote a novel:
Captain Miracle and his Tales.
In truth, there was only one tale,
and only one miracle. But then,
there are only so many tales,
and miracles are getting hard to come by.

He sailed to a distant land,
far down to the end of the first page
where he discovered, and claimed
for his own, no country, no gold
or slaves, but only a donkey.

But it was a magic donkey.
It knew how to speak, and
it only fed on words, so it came
cheap, and Captain Miracle dreamed
and dreamed of how it would make him rich.

But when he returned to his king,
the donkey did not speak one word.
So the king exiled him, and his ass.
Embittered, he returned that donkey
to its profitless home.

But just as the Captain
pulled past the bitter waves
that grew and grew like great fists,
the donkey spoke a single word:
"Goodbye."

And as Captain Miracle faded into white,
he cursed that donkey from the depths
of his empty soul.
It's rather a stupid novel, I think now.
But if Captain Miracle had only listened
to that last, lonely, braying word,
he might have learned a lesson
beyond price.

War of the Magicians

There is this dark magician
appears the night of the emerald moon
each year, determined to
vanquish the heart
of this antique store of dreams.
His evil power-rays of grey
he aims at every color,
every heart of every child
to drain their world of rainbows,
and crave them fear a love of any kind.
So when their bodies grow,
as grow they must, their souls
will turn to rust, or grow
in reverse, like uprooted, upside-
down trees, turned to grey stone,
beneath the stone-grey skies
of the most normal of normal worlds.

I do battle with him,
blocking his death rays
from every fragile glass and child.
I make sure the rocking-horse's eyes
burn forever in the emerald moonlight.
I absorb every color in the store,
like a prism of constellations,
and cast them to children everywhere,
so they never turn into anything
as absurd as a normal world.

The battle ends again; he shrugs again,
in his cape of inky defeat, then departs,
swearing to return when he may some time
capture that emerald moon in his web of envy.
The sun returns like an altar boy
lighting candles one by one,
and all the colors shimmer in joy,
glowing like the fever
in the life of things.

The ghost that was nowhere home

In the closed and locked antique store
one night,
someone crying—no—sobbing—
a woman's suffering pain, I think—
uncertain—the woe is so deep
and blind—
it almost seems inhuman…
Like someone stabbing
a vacuum cleaner bag
with an icepick.
Is it I? Am I dreaming?
Am I still that "troubled" boy?

But my grandmother comes, and now
she hears it too—that awful wound
in the dark or of the dark—
"Why is it here?" I ask.
"Not it, she," my grandmother whispers.
"I've heard her before, on lonely nights.
Perhaps the happy people of day
have outlawed mourning, so now
the ghosts have nowhere to go.
Or perhaps they cut down all the trees
they used to cling to in the wind,
and now she tends her pain alone."

Can we—dare we—open the door and look?
"No, no, we mustn't," she warns. "If we do,
she may shatter like glass. She is pure

as the silenced colors in that store
of dreams and memories, and this
is her only home…No, no, son, let her
be, let her be, but as long as she is here,
you must learn to tend her every tear,
hear her voice in the windspeaking trees,
and then you will learn to love."

The antique children

The antique children
are lined like convenient deaths
on a Victorian loveseat
in my grandmother's store in the country.
Their eyes are jewels that glitter sinister moons.
apricot cheeks, but foreheads cracked with time,
their smiles smothered long ago, lips parted, mouthing
a silence—plump, prettied, and alone.
I believe they are gifted, clued to the dark,
hands clutching an emptiness like fool's gold.
Have they ever touched daylight?
Is there some memory they cannot say?
Late at night I hear them
walking from aisle to aisle,
awkward, desperate as asylum echoes,
searching for any door.
I cover my ears and try not to scream,
as their intricate fingers claw at the lock,
while their rocking horse, strung from the ceiling,
rides away, rides away, rides away…

My grandfather's watch

His grandfather, a minister,
carried it all through the Civil War
as he ministered to the dead or wounded.
Floral patterns adorn the outside,
hand-engraved with precisioned grace.
Click the top—it opens like a bank door.
Inside, Roman numerals stand watch,
guarding a trace of eternity.
Its maker: "American."
It weighs heavy but firm,
like a family tradition
that winding brings to life.

It would be all beauty
if not for the old, old blood
staining the inside cover.
I have tried and tried
to wash it away, will it away.
No use. It will keep its blood forever.
It hoards its own wordless speech,
every horror it has trapped in time,
sending the past round and round.

I wear it in my shirt pocket,
ticking over my heart, gold
and silver, sure and patient.
Awaiting a stray bullet
from that old, old, blood-soaked war,
still searching for a victim.

Night chimes

For the first time
you have set the time
of the Grandfather clocks,
the one in the living room
with silver pendulum,
the one on the stairway landing
the size of a barn owl,
and others and others around the house,
locking old duties with your golden key.
And now the chimes come one at a time
around midnight—deep, sonorous,
echoing night and ancient faith,
like a crow circling a church bell-tower,
followed by another, then another,
alighting time with your secret mission.
But what secret?
Only you know.
All I know: In your room
next to mine
you chant prayers in your sleep
as the cobalt moon outside my window
awakens our memories into song,
and falling oak leaves dream the lonely wind.

Time's hundreds

I sneak into her bedroom
while she is downstairs
reading Shakespeare
and painting Ophelia.
Her room is filled with strangers
in gilt frames. Here is a young man
in a bright new uniform, beaming,
his arm around a fellow soldier.
Can this possibly be my grandfather?
I knew him old, old,
bent like a crumpled cigarette,
drawn down towards bitter earth.
And all these others, round and round.
If I can place them in a sequence,
will they tell his story? No.
There are far too many of him
frozen in too many times
long ago, and now a long
row of soldiers, with dates
carefully written above some of the faces.
I cannot imagine my gentle grandfather
ever shooting anyone. Yet here he is—
the same bright stare, the same
searching eyes. An impostor?
And can this be my grandmother?
How many there are of her!
Hitting a softball, just a girl, an old woman
locked somewhere within her.
Here he lifts her high to an apple tree

in a photo I would study in later times.
She is happy. What is happy?
It is so hard for me to know.

As I see more and more
of these moments in time,
a swirl swoons through me
and I drop to my knees.
How many lives had they lived
before they ever heard of mine?
How could they be grandparents,
these lovers locked in eternal youth?
It is a room filled with strangers
who somehow know me, body,
blood, and bone. I am alone,
yet held here in gentle love.
Are they actors? Puppets? No. They
simply fully inhabit
a world not my own. I float through darkness,
dreaming of other worlds.
I awake long later. I can feel
her gentle hands carry me
to my bed, pull up the covers,
and lay me down to sleep.

The keys

My grandmother's keys
were large, silver and gold,
strung round a long wire chain
weighted with possibilities.
Passwords, I believed,
to a hundred secret rooms.
I took them one day,
and Aliced every door in the house—
no magical dream gardens.
But in the antique store they worked,
and I opened a door in the kaleidoscope air,
and long ago turns sudden into light.

I see my mother, a twelve-year old girl,
and the antique store a grocery store again,
pink scent of bologna in the air.
A Roma places a black hat
with sunburst and blue-gold ribbon
on her head. She laughs and says,
"Oh Father, do let's trade some
sweet potatoes for this?"
I cannot tell if this is memory
or imagination, real or illusion.
All is vision.
I see my grandfather
cutting and carving a rocking chair,
sanding and smoothing the seat and arms,
his fingers as rough and finely etched
as cicada shells, his arms tightly muscled.

A group of farmers surrounds the radio,
and my grandfather leaves for the kitchen,
where he tells my Grandmother: "I consider
myself a gentleman, but I simply cannot
abide that damned Father Coughlin."

What have I heard, when have I dreamed?
I don't know anymore. I only know
I am no longer afraid of time.
I want to wind up every clock
in the store, and set it free to motion.
And still they come these dreams or memories,
glimpses, images formed and dissolved
as quickly as rain patterns down a windowpane.
And finally my grandmother says:
"There are millions here, each
with a story to tell."
I touch each glass, each vase, each clock,
every object of love and loss,
until darkness opens into song.

A distant Shiloh in the night

They have built a Drive-In Theater,
The Shiloh, a mile or so away.
Chrome-grillwork-grimaces under stars
above the radiating screen, the light
escaping it a silk-gloved hand
clutching at the moon.
We laugh at it in wonder—
the jumbled kaleidoscope of colors
shattered and scattered
through our innocent fields,
since the angry men there
talk and talk, and yell, and point,
yet say nothing.
Now come the soldiers, an endless army
of green that lizards treetop to treetop,
then blood turns the moon ruby-red,
and our laughter comes to a halt.
How are we to know,
in our cricket-hidden, firefly love,
that this nightmare exploding far away
is made of coming attractions?

The Party Line

"Listen! Can't you hear?
Someone's listening in on us.
Someone who won't mind their business."
The Party Line was
six houses on one phone line.
The Party Line was
mind your own business.
We are separate,
not a village.
The clue:
If you picked up another conversation,
the phone made clicks like nervous crickets.
The Party Line was
gossip all you want,
but give nothing away.
Use as many words as possible
to say as little as possible
of what you fear or long for.
But mind your own damn business.
I broke the Party Line.
I was listening.
I was always listening.
Listening for secrets
of all their hidden lives,
listening for the silence
between the lies.
Sometimes I would lift the receiver
and try to call myself,
hoping someone would listen and ask me why.

The storm sweeper

"Take a look out the window."

I pull back the curtain to reveal
a world draped in sun and white,
and my grandmother is outside
before I can say one word,
sweeping the unfolding snow
from the front porch
with her usual brisk efficiency,
her toothpick moving in her mouth.
Plumes of snow the size of foxtails
race across the yard, leap the fence
and escape in mid-air.
Now she's sweeping the front walk free.
She sweeps and the wind blows.
She sweeps and the snow comes to life.
She sweeps to the bottom of my heart.

Endgame

I risk the Queen's Gambit
she taught me a year ago.
You sacrifice a pawn
to gain time,
as this is a game
of time and momentum,
and the force of clean lines of attack.

Always before I would find my lost-lorn king
alone and helpless in the corner,
my deranged forces in despair.
Her genius was appearing to attack
with no apparent plan.
It would come clear
only when it was too late
to counterattack,
my imaginary Maginot Line
outflanked and overwhelmed.

It was something about patterns,
secret plans and hidden relations
she always saw before I did.

My grandfather carved the board and pieces
long before I was born,
the king sceptered but lazy,
the queen calm in her power,
knights daring the day,
castles eyeing advantage,

bishops with arms crossed
as if hiding their dark desires.
Her pieces are ebony,
dark as their intentions.
Mine are off-white,
but pure,
like the weathered sands
of Catawba Island.

I move, she moves,
the battle is met.
But this time something is wrong.
I see her once-sure fingers shaking
just a little, as she moves her
forces, she seems tired and worn
like this old board of wounds.

When she presses her king face down,
and shakes my hand, I cannot believe
in my victory. "Even Napoleon
could not have done it better,"
she whispers, then leaves for bed.
I remain a long, long time,
counting the night down
breath by breath. I would rather
she had shaken the board
like a wayward child,
and scattered the armies to free.

In one mere year
have I grown stronger,
or she weaker?
Or both?

Or has my strength sapped hers
like some vampire from ages past?
I feel guilty for being born.
Come back, love, and
we will reset the pieces
and begin forever again,
opening and opening,
only opening, no endgames
or final battles of doom,
frozen here in timeless peace,
and say amen to war evermore.

Departure

Night. The wind cool.
We walk to the well,
my left hand clutching pebbles,
my right hand in your hand.
I no longer need to drink the water
of the well to cure my fevers.
They are long gone.
Slowly, your hand fades from mine,
and you turn to stardust
blown through the countless air.
Now you are all the night sky, my love,
where you will dance and spin forever.

I knew a world once deeply in its wounds

A candle, a sail, a vigil,
I kept the hours gently and well.
Honey bees festooned the breeze,
and I was the strength and faith of days.
Then one morning, I blindly waved a wand
of dandelion seeds. They tumbled down a wind,
drunken, each suddenly lost and alone, and
time awoke, wound up the sun.
The air gasped like a smothered candle.
Treetops grasped at fleeing angels.
Something came accusing the rose,
and the afternoon sighed with butterflies.
I plunged deep in the trees and gardens
and pulled out webs and roots of wounds.
Everything bled tears or dreams or words,
and the cricket's call shivered through the stars.
I followed a child's cry and found it was my own.
Still, I remember how that final sparrow
sank deep within November winds.

Thieves of time

They have descended
from parts unknown.
Relatives my mother has never met
or heard of before.
She dubs them
"The weary of relativity."
They circle the store,
caressing its "curios,"
deaf and blind to every memory.
They seem to float, as if
carried in mists like vampires.
Now they creep, crawl, poke, probe,
pull, tug, yank, clutch to possession.
They cry, cluck, cackle, grunt, gobble,
hiss, gossip and giggle. A beast fable.
I watch their eyes.
They glow like dying stars.
My mother holds her mother's
accounting book. She had hoped
for some kind of auction.
No deal. Hopeless. I know her.
She can no more haggle
or drive a hard bargain
than a cat can bark.
She is herself an antique,
who taught me courtesy,
please and thank you, "Negro,"
"Sir" and "Mamn."

Now their action is done, the battle ended.
The store is stripped of all its history,
and there is no money anywhere.
Each of them simply staked a claim
and ran off with it clutched in their hands.

They leave behind them
only my mother's tears,
her family devotion,
and her impeccable manners.
Outside the empty front store window
winds blow deep and golden through the corn.
And you can tell the wheat, so inspired,
wishes it could run, or fly to distant skies.
And above the front door mantle, a sign:
"Beautiful to look at, delightful to hold,
but if you should break it,
then it is sold."

The magic swing

Of all the swings in the world,
this one was mine alone,
since I knew all its secrets.
It heard all the oceans in the trees,
and traced the quest of fireflies, and
it could swing me among clouds and birds
whose wings and cries trembled the blue,
or it would swing me low to brush the weeds
where an almond light of fireflies
kept vigil through the dusk and dark.
Its chains freeing me from fear
and gravity, and if a day was wrong,
back I'd swing, until breezes
draped starlight through the trees,
and that day had never been,
and if the day was right,
up I'd swing, eyes closed in song,
into the yielding night,
and that day was forever.
Then one day for no reason I knew
I leapt to final earth, letting go
the stars and skies, and church bells
went oh well, oh well…
and the night's harp went silent, the only
sound crickets throbbing in the garden.

Years later, weighted with time,
I found that magic swing again,
filled with the laughter of a boy
I could not recognize, offering me
a password I'd forgotten long ago.

Insofar

Now, years and years later,
the old watch of blood and gold
whispers to me late at night.
It says we're both still here,
are we not? And we both
need to believe in something.
It is right. We're both a bit outworn,
yet enduring, battered but damn stubborn,
ticking our time down to silence.
Insofar as we are both survivors
for now, anyway, and we have learned
to forgive each other's wars.
Insofar as we're in so far,
we may as well live, accepting
what we know we can never know.

Osiris in Ohio

Gathering scattered twigs,
and dropping yew leaves behind me
until the mind is clear and bare
under the weeping willow
sunshade as it blends
into the browning grass
that chants and chants to the west wind:
Mystery, come again.
The new moon dreaming of bones,
the corn rows lined in mourning,
the autumn mists come ghosting, ghosting,
the acorn dreams of the oak,
and I pray come again, come all again,
gather me back in love and memory.

Song of innocence and experience

Once upon a time I sang the sunlight,
and God was a whisper
hidden in the things of Him.
Twenty years later I return,
and everything is gone.
Everything.
The store is a mere stone
foundation. Used car lots
metastasize in our fields.
The sun shattered, moon
pulverized to broken skeletons,
leaving only the invisible.
And vanity, vanity of certainty
spun round in wind, of good people
gone to a thousand lost mornings.
And yet I am strong.
My veins flex like steel cables.
My fear the size of a grain of dust.
You grew me well.
You taught me the grace of others,
and the mindlessness of wars.
So I sit down here with pen in hand
to somehow begin to dream again,
and weave a world from loss and memory.

Proust was right

I am staring out the window
of the Nowhere Motel
as the highway headlights
descend like vultures with cobalt eyes
or needles longing to blind me.
Suddenly I am gone.
Where?
Darkness. Then a soft light.
An antique rocking chair embraces me.
It smells of pipe smoke and rosin.
A radiant dragonfly awaits me
from the small umbrella sky of a Tiffany lamp.
Keys: gold and silver, strong from a strong nail
on a door, weighted with possibilities.
The door opens and I am saturated
with the salty scent
of cured beef.
And now I can see:
A row of old clocks,
each stopped at its own private hour,
grasping one moment forever.
Shelves of glittering glass, all the colors
of the xylophone, iridescent
in moonlight and silence
that hover in expectation like a prayer.
I am a child again, waiting
in my grandmother's store in the country
for my parents to return me home

for a while, until my every breath
longs to return here again
to this store that I love, with its Tappan stove,
strings of strung cigars,
and glimpses of old time.

My grandmother rocks in her chair next to me
as we eat our sandwiches and drink hot chocolate,
and watch the gentle headlights probe up the hill,
casting chevron angels on the sky.
We play our game to guess which lights
will be theirs, this strange destiny.
Then time leaves its memory for mine,
and I am blessed by light and will never be alone.

The invisible cicada

I have wrapped my love round a cicada shell.
I do not know why.
But this shell is the mold of an inner world
that knows its place in time.
The invisible cicada's chant
pulses through my veins
its cry of infinite longing, and heaven
is the silence between its calls.
At night the shell encloses the stars,
and becomes a glowing moon.
By day it is a ring of the sun, reflecting
all color, Christmas on earth.
What am I now but its lonely song,
cast through the thriving fields,
searching for the mystery that
made this double, this careful copy,
into the prison that set it free.

The visitor

The cicada dies and remains
clutched to my upstairs screen window,
punctuating thought.
At dawn it glows gold,
a hyacinth
lit from within
by emptiness,
wings shedding needles of light
to thread the windy leaves.
At noon it burns blue,
folding the sky in its wings.
Living locusts
trill for its return,
but it remains
loyal to its death.
At night it is a black heart
feigning invisibility,
patient,
no longer fearing the cat.
In Summer it remembers
the last cry of its wings.
The storm comes, quickening shadows,
tormenting the screen,
but still it clutches here,
whirling with the earth.
In Winter, winds
turn trees to claws,
but still it clings, waiting,
molding itself

into a diamond of ice.
In Spring it is gone.
Finally, I can leave this house
to find
on my grandmother's tombstone
a cicada shell broken and free.

www.ingramcontent.com/pod-product-compliance
Lightning Source LLC
LaVergne TN
LVHW092023190726
843493LV00002B/563